THE OFFICIAL RSPCA PET GUIDE

D0237515

Care for your Hamster

CONTENTS

Collins

Published by William Collins Sons & Co Ltd
London · Glasgow · Sydney · Auckland · Toronto · Johannesburg

© Royal Society for the Prevention of Cruelty to Animals 1983, 1990

NEW EDITION
First published 1990
9 8 7 6 5 4 3 2 1
This is a fully revised and extended edition
of *Care for Your Hamster*, first published in 1983
and reprinted 6 times

Text of the 1983 edition by Tina Hearne; text
revisions and additions for this edition by Margaret Crush

Designed and edited by Templar Publishing Ltd.,
Pippbrook Mill, Dorking, Surrey

Cover photographs by Sue Streeter
Text photographs by W. Bousfield, John Clegg, Bruce Coleman Ltd,
Jude Evans, Michael Harris, C & L Nature (Cyril Laubscher), Sue Streeter,
Sally Anne Thompson

Illustrations by Mike Woodhatch/David Lewis Artists and
Fred Anderson/Bernard Thornton Artists

A catalogue record for this book is available from the British Library

Printed in Italy by New Interlitho, Milan

ISBN 0 00 412545 2

First things first, animals are fun. Anybody who has ever enjoyed the company of a pet knows well enough just how strong the bond between human and animal can be. Elderly or lonely people often depend on a pet for their only company, and this can be a rewarding relationship for both human and animal. Doctors have proved that animals can be instrumental in the prevention of and recovery from mental or physical disease. Children learn the meaning of loyalty, unselfishness and friendship by growing up with animals.

But the commitment to an animal doesn't begin and end with a visit to the local pet shop. It's a commitment for the whole of that animal's lifetime – anything up to 20 years of total responsibility for its health and well-being. If you are not prepared for the inevitable expense, time, patience and occasional frustration involved, then the RSPCA would much rather that you didn't have a pet.

Armed with the facts, aware of the pitfalls but still confident of your ability to give a pet a good home, the next step is to find where you can get an animal from. Seek the advice of a veterinary surgeon or RSPCA Inspector about reputable local breeders or suppliers. Do consider the possibility of offering a home to an animal from an RSPCA establishment. There are no animals more deserving of loving owners.

As for the care of your pet, you should find in the following pages all you need to know to keep it happy, healthy and rewarding for many years to come.

Responsible ownership means happy pets. Enjoy the experience!

DAVID WILKINS
Chief Veterinary Officer, RSPCA

Introduction

At the beginning of this century, the golden hamster was thought to be extinct. In 1930, however, an exciting discovery was made; a female and her young were found in the Syrian desert. They were taken into captivity for breeding, and became the ancestors of the huge number of laboratory and pet hamsters which have since been reared throughout the world.

Hamsters still retain their place among the most popular pet rodents. They have proved themselves attractive, undemanding, clean, and easily tamed. Potential owners must also realize that they are solitary animals, largely nocturnal by nature, and extremely active.

The fact that the Syrian hamster is solitary may be an advantage. It is one of the few pet animals that may properly – indeed must – be kept singly. Owners who attempt to keep two or more adult hamsters together are subjecting them to unwarranted stress, and inviting conflict that invariably results in injury and death. These animals become gentle and tractable with people, but will fight with each other viciously.

In the wild, golden hamsters are nocturnal, or perhaps crepuscular (active at dawn and dusk). In captivity, they may adapt enough to wake during the afternoon, but the principal periods of activity remain the night, dawn and dusk. It is at these times – and therefore often unseen – that hamsters will fight among themselves

Since hamsters are often seen during their daytime rest period, many people make the understandable but quite wrong assumption that they are indolent animals. The reverse is true. Hamsters are highly active during their waking hours, occupying themselves by running on a wheel, climbing, gnawing, grooming, rearranging their bedding – and escaping.

Sometimes two entirely different species, the Chinese and Russian hamsters, are available (see pp.8–9) but, except where otherwise stated, this book is concerned with the golden or Syrian hamster.

The golden, or Syrian, hamster is one of the few pet animals that must be housed singly.

Varieties

SYRIAN (GOLDEN) HAMSTERS

The natural colour of these hamsters is a rich golden brown above, with a white underside. The face is marked with white crescents beneath dark cheek flashes. Since their introduction to Britain in 1931, golden hamsters have been bred so skilfully and so extensively that they now occur in over a hundred colour varieties.

SELF COLOURS

Single-coloured hamsters are known as 'selfs', and the self colours include white, cream, fawn, honey, cinnamon, grey, silver blue, sepia, chocolate, and various shades of the

Grey Syrian hamster

natural golden colour. Each shade, if recognized by the Hamster Fancy breeders' organization, is referred to as a separate breed, the name of which may include the eye or ear colour, as in the **Red-Eyed Cream, Black-Eyed White, Dark-Eared Albino**, and **Flesh-Eared Albino.**

Perhaps surprisingly, there are no black hamsters, despite the optimistic claims of enthusiasts. There are many dark-coated hamsters, but on examination they are found to have lighter bellies, frequently a lighter ring around the eyes, and they do not 'breed true'.

Black-Eyed Cream

MARKED VARIETIES

The marked varieties are the multi-coloured or patterned hamsters. The most commonly seen is the banded variety which has a broad white band across the hamster's back, dividing the self colour into two sections. Banded hamsters are named according to the self colour, as for example, the **Golden Band, Honey Band**, and **Ruby-Eyed Fawn Band** hamsters.

Other marked varieties of multi-coloured or patterned

Russian hamster

Golden Banded Satin

Tortoiseshell and White

hamsters include the **Piebald**, which is broken-coloured with white-spotting; the **Mosaic**, which has one or more dark markings on a pale coat; and the **Tortoiseshell and White** hamster which has three colours including yellow in the coat.

VARYING COAT-TYPES
Golden hamsters have been successfully bred with varying coats, both longer and shorter than the natural form. The long-haired varieties have an appealing, fluffy look and are bred in the whole range of colour varieties. The short-haired form is the satinized hamster with fur that looks and feels rather like velvet. These, too, are bred in the complete range of colours.

SOCIAL HAMSTERS
There has long been a demand from pet keepers for a social hamster which will live peaceably in a colony. Breeders have sought to meet this demand by offering two species of hamster that are known to live in groups in the wild. Both are small animals, less than half the size of the golden hamster, and the colour varieties are limited.

The Chinese hamster *Cricetulus griseus*, despite its common name, occurs throughout much of Eurasia from Siberia to Tibet, and westwards into eastern Europe. This species is now available to pet keepers, and they may be kept in pairs of males or females but should be introduced under the age of six weeks. Colony rearing in the close confines of captivity has not always been successful. Some of the females are highly aggressive and, particularly when they become pregnant, are very liable to attack the males

Piebald

Long-haired variety

Chinese hamster

unmercifully, making it imperative to house them separately.

The Russian hamster *Phodopus sungorus* occurs throughout Russia, Mongolia and China. These little hamsters are proving much more amenable to family life than the Chinese hamster, and are proving increasingly popular.

Hamsters in the Syrian desert

The golden hamster is one of those remarkable rodents able to survive in the desert where temperatures fluctuate wildly between day and night, vegetation is minimal, and rainfall very low. Some dew is formed by the daily variation in temperature, and this is probably the main source of water for desert rodents.

In order to survive, hamsters have to avoid the drying effect of the sun and are, therefore, forced to spend almost all of their time in darkness. They have to sleep underground during the day, only venturing out in the evening as the sun goes down.

The hamsters' main defence against daytime heat, and consequent dehydration, is their habit of burrowing. During the day these animals rest quietly underground, well insulated against high surface temperatures by as much as a metre's depth of soil.

In the evening, hamsters become active and emerge from their own extensive system of tunnels to roam the desert in search of food. Supplies are scant, and thought to consist mainly of dry seeds that are sifted from the desert soil. Sometimes these seeds will be supplemented by greenfood which occasionally becomes available. It is also possible that hamsters take some insect life.

Temperatures in the desert can fall dramatically at night, but the fur-bearing hamster is insulated against this night-time cold. Hamsters are thought to travel long distances, using their cheek pouches to carry food back to the home burrow where it is hoarded in a separate underground compartment.

In this way, hamsters regulate their uncertain food supply; laying in stores in times of relative plenty, and using them in times of shortage.

As far as we know, hamsters are lone animals. Once they reach adulthood, they live a solitary existence, only seeking out a partner for mating. The female tends her young alone, until they are of an age to fend for themselves and establish their own territories.

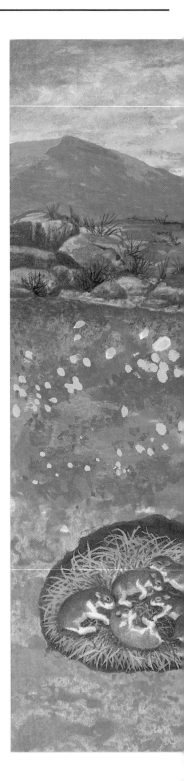

Biology

Colour   As reflected in its Latin name, the natural fur colour of *Mesocricetus auratus* is golden (Latin *aurum*, gold), so it is, therefore, correct to refer to these hamsters as 'golden hamsters'. However, many mutations have appeared in captivity and golden hamsters now occur in a wide range of colours.

Syrian hamster   To avoid the ambiguity of referring to a 'cream golden hamster', it is becoming increasingly popular to call *Mesocricetus auratus* the 'Syrian hamster', following the practice of using geographical names for the other best known species – the European, the Russian and the Chinese.

The golden hamster is not exclusive to Syria, but it is indigenous there and has very strong connections with that country. In 1839 it was first collected and classified by Waterhouse on an expedition to the Syrian town of Aleppo. Almost a century later, when the species was thought to be extinct, another expedition discovered a female with her seven young – again near Aleppo – and took them back to the Hebrew University at Jerusalem. Only three survived captivity (four escaped and one was killed by another hamster) but the three survivors bred so successfully that it was claimed that the entire stock of laboratory and pet specimens was directly descended from the original trio of one male and two female hamsters.

Eyes and eyesight   The bright, beady eyes of a healthy hamster are strikingly attractive, but its eyesight is poor.

Hamsters are, by nature, burrowing animals. They spend the daylight hours resting underground, and emerge only at dusk to forage for food, which they find by sifting the desert soil with their fore-feet.

Golden hamsters spend most of their life in darkness, and rely very little on their sense of sight which is poorly developed as a result and rather myopic.

Teeth   The long incisor teeth at the front of the jaw grow continuously, as in all rodents, and must be trimmed. The easiest and most natural way to deal with this problem is to keep a gnawing block in the hamster's accommodation, together with unshelled brazil nuts (a particular favourite with most hamsters) and hard food such as raw carrot. Neglecting to take these measures may cause the incisors to become overgrown and interfere with feeding.

A hamster spending a lot of time gnawing the bars of its metal cage may be lacking more suitable objects for gnawing.

Fur   People sometimes question why a desert animal, such as the hamster, should be fur-bearing.

The explanation is that fur acts as an insulator against heat and cold, and desert animals need protection from both extremes of climate.

At night, when hamsters are active, the lack of cloud cover over the desert allows the daytime build-up of heat to escape quickly, causing temperatures to plummet; this means that the days can be very hot, the nights very cold.

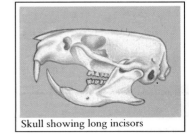

Skull showing long incisors

Scent gland

Golden hamster

Feet and claws The hamster sits up on its hind limbs when feeding, and holds food in the forefeet. The forefeet are also used for pouching and de-pouching food.

The claws tend to become overgrown in captivity, and may need occasional clipping.

Scent gland The dark spots on each hip (which show particularly on the male) are scent glands.

These highly territorial and solitary animals, which spend most of their time in darkness in the wild, are much more dependent on their sense of smell than on their sense of sight.

The scent glands are used to mark territory, but their more particular use seems to be as an aid to finding a mate, for they dry out once the breeding age is passed.

Hibernation The golden hamster is unique because it is the only mammal commonly kept as a pet which also hibernates. Studies have shown that the tendency to hibernate is passed on genetically, and breeders have eliminated the trait as far as possible. Even so, some hamsters will hibernate if kept where they are subjected to a sudden or severe drop in temperature, especially if the temperature change is linked to fewer hours of daylight. In general, the tendency to hibernate is undesirable, for the hamster may not have sufficient stores of body fat to survive, and a sudden awakening can also be dangerous.

Agility Despite the remarkably short tail, the body shape is essentially mouse-like, and the hamster is also mouse-like in its agility.

Those who are now used to seeing a hamster during its active period may be surprised at this talent. A hamster may spend hours sleeping, or will curl up contentedly in a child's hands, but it will also climb curtains, dig furiously, run long distances on an exercise wheel, swing from the bars of a cage, gnaw endlessly, and escape from almost anywhere.

Hamsters deprived of activity in laboratory conditions have quickly succumbed to a stress-linked disease. It seems they fare best when able to attain a high level of activity, and this should be borne in mind when designing hamster accommodation.

Solitary animals The golden or Syrian hamster is a solitary animal. In the wild, the males seek out the females for mating only and stay with them briefly. It has to be recommended that these hamsters should be kept alone in captivity from the age of about five weeks.

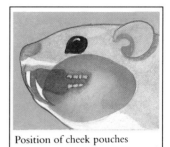
Position of cheek pouches

Cheek pouches The presence of cheek pouches is a remarkable adaptation to a desert habitat. All rodents are able to divide the mouth into two by drawing a fold of skin from the cheeks into the gap (the diastema) between the front and back teeth. In some species, including hamsters, the folds of skin have evolved into permanent cheek pouches which are an important aid to survival.

The pouched rodents are able to eke out an existence in arid country, where food supplies are sparse, by ranging over an extensive area and using the cheek pouches to transport food to their underground hoard.

The habit of hoarding gives rise to the common name 'hamster' which is derived from the German verb meaning 'to hoard'.

A hamster with its pouches stuffed full of seeds can look almost grotesquely puffy around the face, and have a completely different appearance when it has disgorged its hoard into its larder.

The cheek pouches are quite separate from the mouth, and have a rather delicate lining that is easily lacerated by sharp seeds, straw, thistle-heads, softwoods and such like, all of which should be avoided.

Choosing a hamster

SYRIAN, RUSSIAN OR CHINESE?

The popular Syrian is one of the few small pets that must be kept singly, for two or more kept together will usually fight fiercely. *Very* occasionally two of the same sex and from the same litter have been recorded living happily together, but they may turn on each other at any time.

There is one exception: occasionally golden hamsters have been kept successfully in a colony, but only in a very large compound with a series of individual nest areas. It has been found that *given enough space*, golden hamsters will accept community living and communal areas providing each animal has exclusive use of a separate nest area and approach ramp – which is defended jealously.

It is necessary to stress that these successful attempts at colony rearing of adult golden hamsters have taken place in schools and colleges where there are facilities and space available to erect a really large compound. It is very unlikely that suitable accommodation could be provided under normal domestic conditions.

If you wish to keep more than one hamster, seek out a supplier of the little Chinese or Russian (often referred to as Dwarf Russian) species (pp.8–9). The Russians in particular are able to live together peaceably. In most respects the care and requirements of these newcomers is the same as for the Syrian.

Buying a hamster should be a carefully considered decision, and the following points should be noted before rushing out to the nearest pet shop.

Nocturnal lifestyle   Hamsters are normally awake from dusk, through the night, to dawn. They sleep during the day, which is very convenient if the family are out then, but the noise of an exercise wheel can be surprisingly loud and unrelenting at night. Though usually considered a children's pet, hamsters are not always awake when the children are. However, by routinely offering its meal in the

A hamster can be very amusing to watch as it speedily and efficiently pouches its food, though most feeding takes place at night.

mid-afternoon, a young hamster can be acclimatized to rising a little earlier, but the animal should not be woken during the main period of its daytime sleep.

Age It is best to acquire a young hamster so it will soon enjoy being handled and become a good companion. Hamsters have a comparatively short lifespan (p.46), so the younger the animal is, the better. Five to eight weeks is the generally recommended age.

At this age the hamster will probably be nervous. To choose a good pet from a cageful of young hamsters, ignore any cowering in a corner or charging about panic-striken. The most curious hamster should prove the most tamable.

Health A healthy hamster should be plump, with soft, glossy fur over a clean skin, free of abscesses, sores or pimples, and especially of dampness under the tail. See also p.35.

Sex Unless the animal is specially wanted for breeding, its sex is not important, although some people prefer the female's more rounded shape, and others swear that the male lives a little longer. However, if a particular sex is wanted to complete a breeding pair, it is not unknown for pet shop assistants to make mistakes, so do check for yourself.

Variety and colour Fur colour is purely a matter of taste – among the Syrians there are over a hundred combinations. Do not opt for the long-haired variety, though, if you will not have the time or inclination to groom it every other day (p.32).

SOURCES
The best place to buy a hamster for breeding or showing is from a breeder who exhibits regularly at shows. The secretary of the local hamster club should be able to recommend a suitable breeder. However, many perfectly adequate pet hamsters can be acquired from pet shops or from a friend or acquaintance glad to find good homes for surplus youngsters.

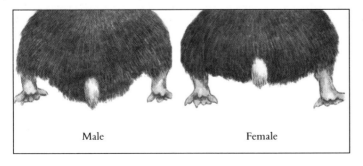

Male   Female

The simplest way of sexing hamsters is by observing the hindquarters, which in the male (left) are tapered and in the female (right) more rounded.

TAKING THE HAMSTER HOME

Have a suitable cage ready *before* you acquire your hamster. This should be warm (hamsters should be kept at a temperature no lower than about 18°C/65°F or they may become dormant) and secure (p.20). The hamster should be carried home in a small ventilated box or tin, with some hay or paper shavings for comfort. Allow it to run from this container into its cage, give it food and water, and leave it entirely alone for 24 hours to settle down. The temptation to peep at it or handle it should be strongly resisted.

'Golden' is an accepted but misleading name for the Syrian hamster, as there are over a hundred colour variations. *L to R*: Black-Eyed White, Golden, Cinnamon, Grey and Fawn.

Blond long-haired variety

Variegated Piebald Syrian

olden hamster and young

Grey hamster

inese hamster

Caging

CHOOSING A SUITABLE CAGE
Since an adult golden hamster is likely to spend its entire life alone in captivity, the owner has a particularly strong responsibility to provide as large and as interesting an environment as possible.

Enough is known about the habits of this hamster in the wild to judge what kind of accommodation is required if the animal's needs are to be met in captivity.

Being an underground creature by nature, with strong nest-building and hoarding instincts, it is vital that the hamster should have some privacy and the opportunity to burrow right out of sight when it chooses. Plenty of bedding and burrowing materials are essential, together with a secluded place for sleeping and hoarding food. Apart from the size of the cage, privacy and the opportunity to burrow are the main requirements of the substitute environment. Any hamster deprived of these comforts would be subjected to an unwarranted amount of stress.

The size of cage is obviously important and, in this respect, a home-made cage may score over a commercially produced one. However, it needs to be said that size alone is not a sufficient guide to the suitability or otherwise of a particular cage. Golden hamsters are very active, and the whole cage interior needs to be accessible if the animal is to enjoy the high level of activity that is natural to it.

Security is a very important consideration. Apart from being highly active and agile, hamsters are also extremely competent at gnawing and will escape from a flimsy or insecure cage. Home-made cages need to be stout enough to withstand constant gnawing, and commercial cages must be securely fastened.

The home-made cage illustrated on pp.22–3 has proved successful in practice. It meets all the requirements listed above and is not difficult to construct. Commercial cages are often suitable providing they are properly used and furnished with sufficient burrowing and bedding materials, with a 'gallery' level added if necessary.

Given a snug home and gentle treatment, a hamster will prove an easy-to-keep and entertaining pet. Since a pet hamster will spend most of its life in the cage its owner provides, it is important that the accommodation be warm and secure, with good use made of the space and offering plenty of opportunities for burrowing and exercise. A cage like that on the right has many drawbacks: it is bare, poorly insulated against the cold and provides no stimulus for an active hamster.

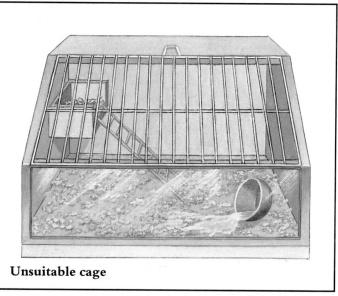

Unsuitable cage

The home-made enclosure

Size Make the dimensions as generous as possible. Overall measurements of **at least** 75 × 40 × 40 cm/30 × 15 × 15 in are recommended.

Wire mesh The wire mesh insert is for ventilation. It also serves as a climbing-frame. The mesh should be securely fixed within a wooden surround. A hamster will work at a weak joint and eventually escape.

Glass top The sliding glass top is to allow good observation and access to the hamster with the minimum disturbance. The glass needs to slide on runners holding it securely in position. If the glass can be lifted at a corner, the hamster will soon escape.

Construction Hardwood is the best construction material, but soft wood with a smooth, laminated plastic finish (such as Formica) is a cheaper and more readily available alternative. The framework will be damaged by gnawing if it is left exposed.

Exercise wheel Most caged hamsters have to rely on a nightly wheel-run for the major part of their exercise. Select a solid wheel, and fix it close to the cage-wall so that the hamster cannot become trapped behind it. Do not use a play ball for the same reason.

Drinking water bottle A drip-feed bottle should be suspended in the cage. Keep the spout clear of the burrowing litter or water will leak from the bottle and make the whole cage damp.

Floor litter The design of this cage makes it possible to provide the hamster with a deep layer of suitable materials for shredding and burrowing.

Put a layer of coarse sawdust or peat (for their absorbent qualities) on the base of the cage. Now add layers of materials such as medicated parchment, kitchen paper, hay and cardboard. Newsprint and magazines should not be used as the inks can be poisonous to hamsters. Cotton wool should not be used either. Leave the hamster to shred and arrange the materials as it wants.

Damp corner

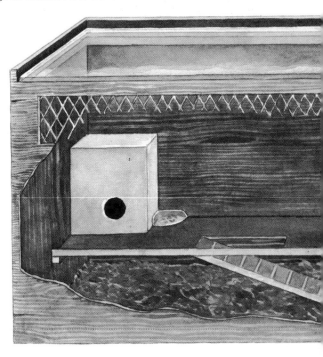

Food bowl

Drinking water bottle

Gnawing block All hamsters need to gnaw, in order to wear down their long incisor teeth. In accommodation such as this, which provides the hamster with plenty of material for shredding, the teeth are unlikely to become seriously overgrown. However, it is still advisable to provide a gnawing block of hardwood, and some hard 'toys' such as unshelled brazil nuts, dog biscuits, and a carrot.

Gallery The raised gallery greatly extends the floor area of the enclosure, and allows the owner easy access to the food containers and damp tray. It also lifts the exercise wheel and water bottle well clear of the burrowing matter.

Food store If the hamster is given such perishable foods as egg, cheese and fish, it will be necessary to inspect the food store every day or two. It is always said that hamsters are quickly upset if their hoard is obviously disturbed, but it is equally important to remove discreetly any decaying food while the hamster is at play elsewhere.

Nest box

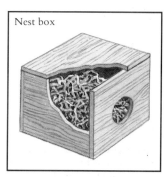

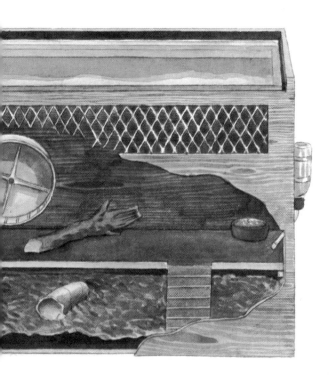

Nesting box Golden hamsters have a very strong nesting instinct. Provide a separate nest box together with soft hay or bedding. (Avoid using synthetic fibres, or any natural fibres such as knitting wools, which may cause obstruction if ingested.)

Occasionally, in very hot weather for instance, the hamster will move its nest. This is usually a temporary move, and the nest box should remain in place.

Exercising

THE NEED FOR EXERCISE

Hamsters need to travel long distances in the wild, in order to collect enough food to survive in desert conditions. In captivity the opportunity to move around is largely removed, together with the urgent need to do so. Yet hamsters will still travel long distances every night on an exercise wheel because the instinct to be active remains. It has been shown that caged hamsters thrive most when given plenty of opportunity for exercise, and the best accommodation is designed with this need in mind.

Enabling the hamster to use all the cubic space available in the accommodation is as important as the overall size. This is why devices such as ramps and galleries, bars for climbing, tunnels, a wheel, and plenty of materials for gnawing, shredding, and tunnelling should be included. Together, they have the effect of extending the confines of the cage and warding off boredom by providing the opportunity for a captive animal to keep itself well-occupied.

EXERCISE WHEEL

A solid wheel is generally preferred to one with open rungs, and it should be fixed close enough to the cage-wall to prevent the hamster becoming trapped behind it.

There has always been some controversy about the

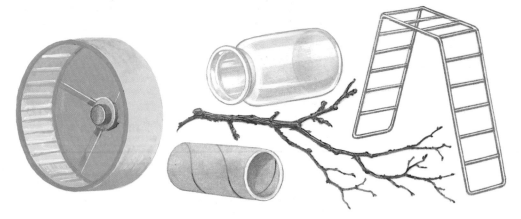

A good adventure playground for a hamster could include an exercise wheel, a jam jar, a toilet roll, a climbing frame, and a small branch.

A wheel such as this, with open rings and spokes, can be dangerous since a hamster may easily trap a limb while the wheel is spinning.

use of exercise wheels for pet rodents, because there are occasional reports of mishaps when animals become trapped in or behind the wheel, usually by a limb or the tail. The hamster, with its almost non-existent tail, is less at risk than some rodents in this respect, and its great need for activity is usually considered to outweigh any slight risk of accident that may be present.

Care should be taken if a female and her young are using a wheel together. The young tend to hurl themselves on the wheel – and on each other – and with each one pulling in a different direction there is, perhaps, an increased risk of accident. For this reason, free-standing wheels are not recommended for use by a young litter.

THE NEED FOR SUPERVISION

Captive hamsters seem to enjoy having a free play-time each day. Some owners give them a bucket of soil to dig in, or allow them the freedom of a room. Like all animals, hamsters vary in temperament. Some will lurk in the shadows behind the sofa; others will make straight for the curtains or the stair carpet – both of which they are able to climb. Some supervision is therefore prudent!

There are, of course, hazards to such a free regime. Hamsters are notoriously quick and agile and frequently become lost. In one school, the hamster disappeared for three months and was found nesting in the dustbag of the vacuum cleaner. Another was lost on moving day but emerged in the new house from a large potted plant!

Sometimes it is possible to recapture an errant hamster in a tall, sloping jar, made comfortable with a ball of bedding material, and baited with food. More usually a lost hamster will give itself away by making a lot of noise.

Feeding

In the wild, the golden hamster is thought to be mainly herbivorous, living on a diet of dry, wind-blown seeds, supplemented with occasional greenstuff, and possibly some small grubs and insects.

In captivity, the hamster thrives best on a diet of mixed seeds, grains and nuts. These may, if convenient, be bought packeted from a reliable manufacturer, and can be supplemented with other cereal foods such as wholemeal bread, puppy meal and porridge oats. Hamsters delight in extracting and pouching tiny fragments of kernel from a pile of nutshells after the main part of the nut has been eaten by its owner.

Hamsters will eat many kinds of fresh fruit and vegetables including apple, pear, tomato, salad greenstuff, cabbage, carrot, swede and wild plants such as well-washed clover, dandelion and groundsel. Plants from roadside verges or from any area that may have been sprayed with chemicals should be avoided. The following are all poisonous to hamsters: coltsfoot, rhubarb leaves, potato tops and tomato leaves.

Favourite titbits include grapes, raisins, fruit cake, whole brazil nuts and sunflower seeds.

Hamsters enjoy a varied diet, the bulk of it being different types of seeds and nuts, much as it would be in the wild.

Some animal protein may be occasionally introduced into the diet by offering slices of hard-boiled egg, pieces of cheese, flakes of cooked fish and small shreds of cooked meat.

It is really only necessary to feed the hamster once a day. The main meal may be offered in the early evening, and later on (or in the morning) some greens, fruit and hard, chewy foods.

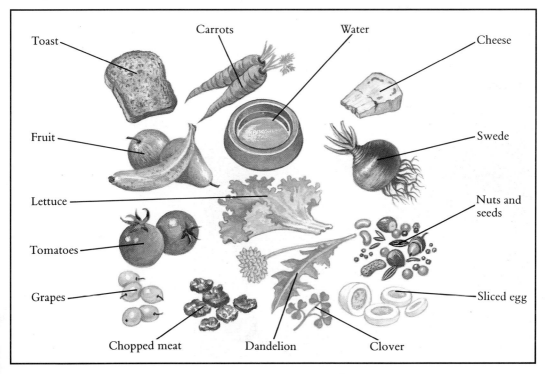

As the hamster is a hoarding animal by nature, most food will be pouched and taken to the food store to be eaten later. Dry foods should be left undisturbed in the store, but perishable foods should be removed, as unobtrusively as possible, before they have time to rot. A hamster's food intake is very small and if perishable food is regularly found hoarded, its rations are probaby over-generous.

Fresh drinking water must always be available. Since an open dish would soon be spilled or filled with cage litter, a drip-feed bottle is recommended. Check that the valve operates freely, and that the hamster does not pile up litter beneath the spout to make the bottle leak. To prevent algae, the water bottle can be painted black, but with the bottom left unpainted to check the water level.

There is no excuse for denying a hamster access to drinking water on the grounds that it is a desert animal. Conditions in the desert are harsh, but the hamster is free there, and well adapted to survive by keeping below ground during the day. In its complex of underground burrows temperatures are equable, much lower than on the surface, and humidity is relatively high. The hamster also has the advantage of the morning dew, and is free to go off in search of green food such as desert succulents, with their high water content.

By contrast, conditions in a cage would soon become intolerable unless the owner understands that, once restricted in captivity, the hamster is entirely dependent on human help to provide sufficient water for its well-being.

Most food is pouched by the hamster and carried off to the store to be eaten later.

Suggested diet chart

	What?	When?	How much?
Adult hamster	mixed seeds, grains, nuts *or* hamster pellets *plus* wholemeal bread, puppy meal and/ or uncooked porridge oats	early evening	about 1 heaped teaspoonful, but offer more for pouching and storing
	fresh fruit and vegetables, and greenstuff well washed in cold water	late evening or morning	as much as hamster will consume the same day
	protein such as chopped hard-boiled egg, cheese, scraps of fish, cooked meat	with either of above meals	in very small amounts, no more than will be consumed the same day
	fresh water	always available	
	milk (preferably *slightly* sour)	liked by many hamsters as part of routine diet, but should *always* be given if dietary deficiency is suspected	
Pregnant and lactating females	As above, but give milk routinely, plus mash of fine oatmeal or baby food with milk. Increase quantities, especially of the protein sources, as her appetite increases.		
Growing young	See p. 43		

Hamster with pouches full (left) and pouches empty.

Handling

Children are sometimes disappointed to find that a newly acquired pet hamster is difficult to catch and may even bite. It needs to be explained that an animal bred by a commercial breeder will have been handled very little prior to being sold. The hamster must be tamed before anyone can handle it confidently and easily.

Taming a hamster just involves accustoming it to being handled, and is usually achieved in the space of a few weeks. It takes only patience, understanding and a little time. Young hamsters are easily tamed, and may safely be touched just before weaning when they emerge from the nest to take solid food. By this time they are unlikely to be attacked by an over-anxious mother. Older hamsters can also be encouraged by gentle treatment to become very tractable and friendly. Food is the way to any animal's heart, but do not point a finger at the hamster to sniff as it may mistake it for food and bite!

To entice a hamster from its nest, place some food in the cage and tap gently on the cage side. The hamster will soon learn to associate the tapping with food.

Whatever the age of the animal, begin the taming process simply with stroking movements, and hand-feeding during the active period. As soon as this much attention is readily accepted without resentment or nervousness, begin to lift the animal by cupping it in the hands. Eventually progress to lifting the hamster by the loose skin at the back of the neck with thumb and finger while supporting the body weight with your free hand at the same time. If you make a tunnel shape with each of your hands in turn, it will wriggle through from one hand to another.

Any hamster may make an unexpected jump if startled, so always handle it over a surface such as a table top for safety. Never let the hamster fall more than about 20 cm/8 in as serious injury is likely. If surprised by a sudden movement from above, the hamster is likely to freeze, and then creep towards cover with its body flattened close to the ground. It should always be understood that, before

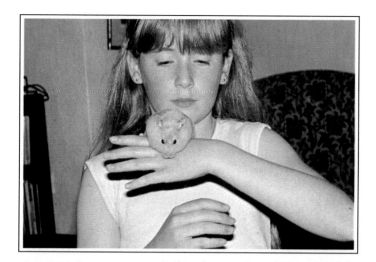

Let the hamster climb from one hand to another, down an endless series of 'steps', and satisfy its desire to keep moving.

Hamsters can move with great agility, so even confident owners should take great care and always handle them over a flat surface in case they fall.

allowing a hamster to exercise out of its cage, it is likely to be ill at ease in an exposed situation and may well make a sudden dart for the cover of the nearest shadow.

Do not disturb a sleeping hamster. However, owners may find that a hamster which has been resting all day in a quiet house will rouse itself in response to the sound of the family returning home in the afternoon.

Grooming and hygiene

SHORT-HAIRED VARIETIES

A short-haired hamster normally grooms itself very thoroughly, and only in exceptional circumstances would it need any assistance from the owner. Just occasionally a hamster may get unusually dirty – after an escapade up the chimney or in the coal cellar, for example. It would then probably need swabbing gently with a pad of cotton wool wrung out in warm water. Take veterinary advice about using detergent or any other substance on a hamster's fur contaminated by oil, for instance. (It is advisable not to allow free play in a garage or similar work area.)

LONG-HAIRED VARIETIES

These hamsters should be groomed regularly, and not only when the coat becomes matted, tangled and dirty. It is suggested that grooming every other day will keep the coat in good order. Use a soft dry toothbrush, dampened with warm water if necessary to restore a neglected or badly soiled coat to its proper condition.

Hamsters are fastidious and very supple animals, able to reach to groom every part of their own body. Long-haired varieties may require brushing every other day.

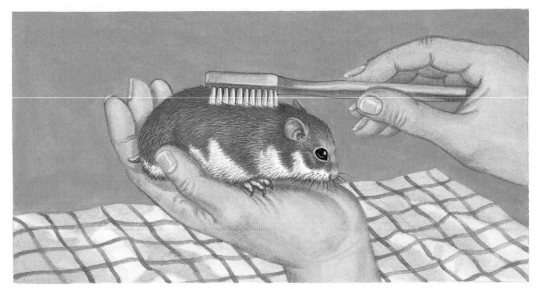

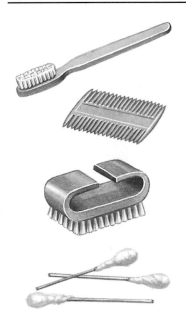

Grooming tools

GROOMING AS A DISPLACEMENT ACTIVITY
When an animal is put into a difficult situation, it will often indulge in an irrelevant, completely disconnected activity that can do nothing to solve the problem, yet seems to relieve the feeling of stress. Biologists call this 'displacement activity', and a human parallel would be a worried person scratching his head or smoothing his hair.

Hamster owners will notice that their pet may also use grooming movements as a displacement activity, indulging in quite unnecessary bouts of grooming when put into a stressful situation such as a totally new environment, a freshly cleaned cage, or in a confrontation with another hamster.

TEETH CLEANING
The teeth can only be cleaned by working them on hard food such as raw apple or carrot, and by gnawing on wood. Provide hardwoods only, because hamsters may pouch splinters of softwood and damage the delicate pouch linings.

Cage hygiene

Traditionally-designed cages need thorough cleaning once a week, and the accommodation recommended on pp.22–3 will need cleaning and refurbishing about every two weeks. The hamster should meanwhile be lodged in a secure, ventilated box.

Each day remove droppings, refill the water bottle, and extract greens and other perishable foods from the cage or, if need be, from the food store. If the bedding is clean, shake and replace it, adding a little more hay. Some hamsters are much more tidy than others, selecting different parts of their accommodation for urinating, defecating, and so on, which makes tidying the cage daily an easier and more effective task.

To avoid making the cage unduly damp, a young or newly acquired hamster can be trained to use a selected 'damp corner'. Any small, rigid plastic tray of sawdust will serve. Alternatively, a jam jar turned on its side or a corner cut from a firm plastic container can be used. If a little damp sawdust is retained and replaced each time the cage is cleaned, the hamster should soon learn by smell to urinate in the same place.

The healthy hamster

Hamsters are basically very healthy little animals if kept in good conditions and fed properly, but prevention of disease is better than cure. It is, therefore, important to look at and handle the hamster every day, in order to become familiar with the animal's appearance when it is well. It should then be much easier to spot any change for the worse. The main external signs of a healthy hamster are listed opposite.

When they do fall ill, hamsters need prompt veterinary attention, in common with all the small mammals which have very poor powers of recuperation.

Anus	clean; no staining, scouring or discharge
Appetite	good; eating well during the active period and hoarding food
Breathing	silent and regular
Body	well-fleshed and rounded; no growths, sores or swellings
Claws	short and trim; no splits
Coat	clean and dry; no soiling, tangling or matting; no parasites
Demeanour	calm, quiet and restful during the day; highly active, quick, alert and agile in active period
Ears	fur-covered when young, balding with age; not torn, no discharge
Eyes	bright and clear; no cloudiness, discharge or encrustation
Feet	strong and well-formed; no deformity, weight distributed evenly
Mouth	clean; no sores or dribbling
Movement	quick, darting movement from exposed situations into shadow; good climbing and burrowing abilities
Nose	clear of any discharge or dried mucus
Pouches	used frequently, filled and emptied with forefeet; no soreness or abnormal swelling
Teeth	clean and undamaged; front incisors worn down naturally on hard food and gnawing blocks

Overgrown teeth If a hamster does not have enough suitable gnawing material, its incisor teeth can become so overgrown that it cannot feed properly. Veterinary help is needed to correct this, after which the hamster must be fed a proper diet (pp.26–9) so the problem does not recur. If the hamster loses one tooth, its opposite number in the other jaw will grow too long and need to be cut at frequent intervals.

Young banded hamsters. Hamsters normally remain free from disease and parasites if they are kept in good conditions and fed a suitable diet. It is important that they are not subjected to any unnecessary stress by having their mainly nocturnal routine disturbed unduly, for they do need quiet and privacy during the morning and early afternoon.

Overgrown claws This usually happens with elderly hamsters. It is possible to trim the claws very carefully with sharp scissors, or the animal nail clippers sold in pet shops, but the claws must be held to the light to make sure no blood and nerve vessels are severed. It is safest to take a dark-coloured hamster to the vet for this procedure.

WHEN YOU ARE AWAY

Because hamsters store their food, it is possible to leave them unattended for a *very short time*, such as a weekend. This is totally contrary to the requirements of other mammalian pets, but hamsters will ration their food instead of gorging their food all at once. Naturally, adequate water must be left for the whole period, and food should not include more perishable foodstuffs than the hamster will eat up completely on the first day. Any food it stores will then be non-perishable.

Ideally someone should come in to feed the hamster, as of course *must* happen if the owner's absence is for a longer period. Leave a note of the hamster's food, water and bedding requirements, together with the vet's telephone number. Keeping the supplies near the cage is helpful. If the absence is for any length of time, the friend or neighbour will have to be prepared to clean out the cage and should be warned how to do this without losing the little animal. If the timespan is short enough, only the damp corner should be cleaned, and the carer advised to leave the hamster in its cage. It is, of course, also possible to board hamsters with a vet or pet shop, or possibly a breeder.

First aid

In an emergency, expert veterinary advice should be sought immediately. The hamster should be picked up carefully and taken to the vet in a small secure container lined with hay. If you are not certain of surgery hours, telephone first to make sure that the veterinary surgeon will be there.

FALLS
Probably the most frequent emergency problem with hamsters is that of a fall. Hamsters have a very delicate bone structure and are short-sighted, so they are prone to accidents. If the hamster seems distressed after a fall, it should be returned gently to its nest and left alone to recover from the shock. If the hamster doesn't seem to have recovered in an hour, or if broken bones or internal injuries are suspected, it should be taken immediately to the vet.

HIBERNATION
Not an emergency, but it is recommended that a hamster found curled up in a hard ball, with shallow breathing (so that it may at first be mistaken for dead) should be revived slowly in the hands, or in a warm room. Hibernation can occur if the temperature in which the cage is kept is too low or drops suddenly.

Hibernating hamster

OVERHEATING
Caged animals like hamsters should never be left in direct sunlight. At temperatures above 27°C/80°F hamsters can become rigid and apparently dead for several minutes. They may also quiver and shake. It may take a few minutes before the animal reverts to normal.

WOUNDS
Small clean wounds will usually heal themselves. Larger ones can be bathed in mild antiseptic, but a vet's advice is preferable, because of the risk of infection and of the abscesses which occur if the upper part of a deep wound heals over and traps dirt or bacteria inside.

Ailments

ABSCESSES AND ULCERS
These usually develop on a wound caused by one hamster
fighting another. If there is a discharge, bathe with a mild
antiseptic solution. Abscesses in the cheek pouches are
more serious, and veterinary help should be sought in
dealing with any abscess or ulcer that makes an animal
unwell or is slow to heal.

CONGENITAL DEFECTS
Certain defects such as club foot and eyelessness may be
passed on genetically. Inexperienced breeders should
understand that such animals must never be used for breeding, and those suffering from a disabling defect should be
destroyed humanely.

IMPACTION OF POUCHES
Sometimes a hamster will pouch unsuitable materials
which cause the cheek pouches to become impacted. Do
not delay in asking a veterinary surgeon to remove the
obstruction.

INFLAMMATION OR ENCRUSTATION OF
THE EYES
Conjunctivitis is a common complaint. It may be associated with upper respiratory tract infections or caused by
an irritant such as sand, grit or dust. Consult a veterinary
surgeon in the early stages of the complaint. It may be,
however, that a hamster which fails to remove an encrustation around the eyes is suffering another sign of ageing. In
this case, help the animal to groom properly by bathing
around the eye with cotton wool wrung out in warm
water.

LOSS OF FUR AND SORE SKIN
Although few hamsters live more than three years, they
show definite signs of ageing. Loss of fur is nearly always
such a sign. The ears go bald first, and then the body fur

around the hindquarters and on the animal's underside. Sometimes the loss of fur is caused by friction, and is usually accompanied by sores. It is necessary to remove the cause of friction, at least temporarily. Hair loss and irritation may also be associated with skin parasites such as mites, or, occasionally, ringworm fungus. If in doubt, seek veterinary advice.

POISONING BY AEROSOL SPRAYS

Since hamsters spend so much time grooming, they are particularly at risk if poisonous sprays are used in the same room. Check the manufacturer's instructions concerning pets in the room before using a spray, or temporarily remove the hamster's accommodation until any airborne residue has settled.

Never use poisonous sprays in the same room as a hamster

RESPIRATORY DISORDERS

Upper respiratory infections (colds) can occur, causing sneezing and catarrh, with sore nose and eyes. It is believed that hamsters may be susceptible to human cold and influenza viruses. Pneumonia, with laboured breathing, can develop as a serious complication. Damp or draughty living conditions and poor nutrition encourage respiratory infection. Good nursing and a suitable environment are essential, and additional veterinary treatment may be necessary.

Another cause of respiratory disorder can be dusty or musty hay (or other bedding or burrowing materials), to which the animal may develop an allergic reaction.

WET TAIL

A highly infectious disease of the bowel thought to be associated with stress, e.g. sudden change in the diet and/or environment. Wet tail quickly spreads, and is dreaded by those who keep a large hamstery.

The non-specific early symptoms are a general loss of coat condition, listlessness, and a lack of interest in food. These are followed by characteristic watery diarrhoea from the anus. This makes the fur around the tail constantly wet and accounts for the name of the disease.

Prompt veterinary attention must be sought, but even so wet tail is often fatal. Strict hygiene is necessary, particularly if the cage or its accessories are to be re-used, or if more than one hamster is kept, even though they are in separate cages.

Reproduction

A female hamster will probably produce between five and seven young at a litter, and within two months of their birth each will need a separate cage! So it is essential to know good homes can be found for them all before even thinking of mating any hamsters.

Since most owners only keep one hamster, the question of breeding does not normally arise, and certainly breeding by amateurs cannot be recommended. If breeding is considered seriously, plenty of advice should be taken first, if possible from several experienced breeders.

Syrian hamsters are difficult to pair-up even for mating and, unless conditions are right, the female will turn on the male in a most aggressive fashion. She may inflict serious injuries on him if they start to fight.

A female will never allow a male into her own territory, and is rarely receptive in his. The only way is to introduce them on neutral ground – new to them both – and unless she shows some sign of being receptive quickly, to separate them again before fighting can begin.

It is wise to supervise the session wearing stout gloves, so that they can be parted by hand if necessary.

When the female is receptive to the male, which will nearly always be in the evening during the natural period of activity, leave them together for about 20 minutes – this is quite sufficient. When the female is unreceptive, abandon the session and try the pairing again on several consecutive evenings, remembering that she comes into season every fourth day.

As a member of a solitary species, the female will rear her young entirely alone, with no help from the male who must be taken from her immediately after copulation, and with no help from humans, whose interference she is likely to resent.

The female should be provided with plenty of extra bedding and nesting materials such as soft hay in her own accommodation. She will construct a nest which may be open-topped during a hot spell.

She also needs to be given plenty of fresh drinking water since pregnant animals usually drink more than usual, and she will benefit from having milk at this time. Her normal diet should be increased in amount and quality. In particular, increase the protein – including the animal protein – in her diet. She will need this extra nutrition during pregnancy and lactation.

Breeding puts a great strain on the female, both physically and mentally, since she has the entire responsibility for her litter which may amount to a dozen or more and is invariably boisterous.

Although it is usual for males to become sexually capable of breeding during their sixth week, and females during their eighth week, breeding is best postponed until a minimum age of 12–14 weeks is reached.

A professional breeder would expect a female to bear no more than three litters during her breeding life, which lasts until she is twelve months old. To prevent her becoming exhausted and bearing litters of poor quality, it is essential that she be rested between each family.

If, as is usual, the first litter is conceived when the female is about three months old, the second should not be conceived before the age of six months, and mating for the final litter should be delayed until the female reaches the age of nine months.

The female should be provided with plenty of extra bedding to construct a nest, which may be open-topped in hot weather (as shown).

The young

Syrian hamsters have the shortest gestation period of any mammal, lasting only sixteen days. As a result of this brief pregnancy the young are born very immature – blind, furless and completely helpless. By seven days fur has developed, though usually paler than it will be on the adult animal.

Litters tend to be in the range of 5–7 young, but much bigger litters of 14–17 are not unknown. Most female hamsters of this species bear 14 nipples which is an indication that large litters are usual. However, a litter of 14 young would weigh not more than 28 g/1 oz.

Experienced handlers will lure the female away from the young in order to inspect a young litter, but this is always chancy since newborn hamsters are at risk from attack by their own mother if she or they are disturbed. It is safer for a novice breeder to forgo observing the very early stages of development. The droppings tray should be cleaned every day, but the nest left alone unless it absolutely *has* to be examined. Then the fingers should not be used, but the top of the nest can be opened slightly with a piece of wood

Young hamsters are social animals, but should be housed individually from 5–6 weeks old.

rubbed in cage litter. The female should have first been removed, and then distracted with food when she is returned to the cage.

The female has to tend her litter entirely alone, since Syrian hamsters are not family animals. Early growth is rapid, and the young may be expected to emerge from the nest during the second week of life, when they will begin to take solid food such as fine oatmeal, puppy meal and finely chopped greenstuff.

By the age of three or four weeks, the young will have completed the transition to solid food. They are likely to be quite independent by the end of the fourth week, and sometimes earlier.

If the mother shows signs of being exhausted or exasperated, the young may be removed from her as soon as they have been weaned, and live together in a colony for a further week or two.

At five to six weeks, as they begin to reach puberty, the rough and tumble play of the young will turn to real fighting, and they will be liable to mate each other. It is therefore essential that after this time each hamster should be housed individually.

The females tend to be noisier and more aggressively territorial than the males, but either sex is delightful. These solitary animals are more than usually dependent on their owners, but if your lone hamster is given good living conditions, the opportunity to exercise and plenty of attention, it will prove to be an engaging pet.

Your questions answered

Is it all right to feed my hamster small sweets as an occasional treat?
Very definitely no! Food foreign to any animal's diet can cause an upset stomach and, if fed in excessive quantities, death.

In the wild, hamsters feed mainly on seed, grain and, when they can find it, vegetable matter. In captivity their diet should reflect this, and on p.29 there is a table which lists a variety of suitable food. For a treat, try giving your hamster a grape, some sultanas, or perhaps a tiny chunk of hard cheese to gnaw on. Never be tempted to see whether it likes things like sweets and chocolate – even a small piece represents a large amount to such a tiny animal.

Whenever I try to pick up my hamster, it bites. Am I doing something wrong?
Probably the hamster is scared of you and trying to protect itself. If you are patient, you should be able to overcome this. Start by simply stroking the hamster and hand-feeding it when it is active. When it no longer seems to resent this or to be nervous, try lifting it by cupping it in your hand. Eventually you should be able to lift the hamster by the loose skin at the back of the neck, while supporting the body weight with your other hand.

Why does my hamster spend hours gnawing at his cage?
Basically boredom. Give him plenty of opportunities for exercise and interesting things to do.

How can I make a room hamster-proof? I like to let mine out to run around, but she always seems to find a way to escape.
There's no magic formula, except to say that hamsters can find their way into very tiny gaps, and also climb and jump higher than you'd ever imagine. If, despite your best endeavours, the hamster keeps disappearing, try watching

her like a hawk all the time she is out, to find out *exactly* where she goes. You may then discover her escape route. However, do not worry overmuch if she does disappear temporarily. She will usually return, especially if you put the open cage on the floor with some food inside.

A neighbour's hamster recently died of hypothermia. What precautions should I take to avoid mine going the same way?

For a start, don't let the room which houses the hamster's cage become too cold; if there is any danger on a chilly night, move the cage into a warmer area. If your precautions fail and the hamster appears dead, he may have gone into hibernation. Try warming him up with a hairdryer (kept on the move so it doesn't burn him).

Can you train hamsters not to soil their bedding? Mine never seems to use the tray provided.

Some hamsters seem to be tidy, others not. Try cleaning out the cage very thoroughly, and put a small amount of soiled litter back in the area you want used as a toilet. With luck, the hamster will catch on. Alternatively, are you cleaning the cage out frequently enough? If it is smelly all over, the hamster is unlikely to distinguish between his bed and his lavatory.

When I clean out my hamster's cage, I am surprised to find how much food he has stored in his nesting box. Some of it had gone mouldy. Am I feeding him too much?

Yes!

My grand-daughter longs for a pet of her own. Would a hamster be a suitable Christmas present?

No pet, large or small, should *ever* be given as a surprise present, especially at Christmas. There is too much noise and excitement, and no time to introduce the animal quietly and carefully. The young animal may be nervous, pining for its mother and siblings, and what it needs is absolute peace and quiet. Also, Christmas is a bad time to buy a hamster. Relatively few animals are born in winter and those that are in the shops may have been weaned too early, to catch the Christmas trade. Finally, see p.14 – a hamster is not necessarily an ideal pet for a small child, owing to its nocturnal habits. A gerbil might be better.

Life history

Scientific name	*Mesocricetus auratus*
Gestation period	16 days (average)
Litter size	5–7 (average)
Birth weight	$2g/\frac{1}{14}oz$ (average)
Eyes open	12 days (approx.)
Weaning age	21–27 days
Puberty	45–60 days
Adult weight	100g/3½oz (average)
Best age to breed	12-plus weeks (see p.41)
Oestrus (or season)	every 4 days
Duration of oestrus	4–23 hours (typically persists for an evening)
Retire from breeding	males 15 months females 12 months
Life expectancy	18 months–2 years average (males tend to outlive females)

Record card

Record sheet for your own hamster

(photograph or portrait)

Name HARRY.

Date of birth
(actual or estimated) APPROX. FEBUARY 91.

Breed SYRIAN.   Sex M.

Colour/description TAN AND
WHITE WITH SPOTS
OF BLACK.

Feeding notes HAMSTER MIX
WITH ADDED PEANUTS.
LETTUCE, CABBAGE,
GRAPES, CHEESE,
APPLE, CARROT,
WATER.

Medical notes

Veterinary surgeon's name

Practice address EQUI PET 24 NICOL STREET
KIRKCALDY FIFE SCOTLAND

Surgery hours BY
APPOINTMENT

Tel. no. 641333

Index